THANKS FOR NOTHING, HIPPIES

SARAH CLANCY

salmonpoetry

Published in 2012 by
Salmon Poetry
Cliffs of Moher, County Clare, Ireland
Website: www.salmonpoetry.com
Email: info@salmonpoetry.com

ISBN 978-1-908836-01-4

COVER ARTWORK: © *Jaminsonmoses* | *Dreamstime.com*
COVER DESIGN: *Siobhán Hutson & Jessie Lendennie*

Salmon Poetry receives financial support from
The Arts Council / An Chomhairle Ealaíon

For the emigrants Eimear, Paul & Maire

100% Extra Free

This this one one time time only only we we
offer offer twice twice as as much much poetry poetry
for for the the same same low low prices prices
in in fact fact you you will will find find this this
excellent excellent value value own own brand brand
book book of of poems poems beats beats all all
other other books books of of similar similar quality quality.
Please please keep keep your your receipt receipt
refunds refunds or or exchanges exchanges
will will not not be be entertained entertained
without without proof proof of of purchase purchase.
Terms terms and and conditions conditions apply apply.
Offer offer does does not not effect effect
your your statutory statutory rights rights.

Acknowledgements

Some of these poems have appeared in the following publications: The Poetry Bus, Anthology One-Doire Press, Cuadrivio Magazine, Revival, The Stony Thursday Book, Wow Anthology, Stacey and the Mechanical Bull-Lapwing Press and The Irish Left Review.

Huge thanks are due to everyone who helped and encouraged me with this collection and there are many, but in particular thanks to Tadhg Mc Grath, to Kevin Higgins and Susan Millar DuMars of Over the Edge, Elaine Feeney, James Joyce, Aoibheann Mc Cann and Miceal Kearney who all read drafts of this collection for me, to John Walsh and Lisa Frank, to all the members of the Galway Arts Centre Thursday Afternoon Group, to Dennis Greig for being a legend in general, to Dave Lordan, William Wall and Steve Murray for encouragement, to Kevin O'Shea for the author photo, and of course to all the Facebook friends who have been tormented with drafts of these poems over the last two years.

Particular and especial thanks to Jessie Lendennie and Siobhán Hutson of Salmon Poetry for all they have done and continue to do for the likes of me.

Contents

Horse Thief

I come from a long line of robber barons
with a great welcome for myself,
I'll eat your food, drink your wine
then I'll set your crops alight
and vanish to the mountains with
your horses and cattle charmed and
walking so light-footed behind me
that you won't have heard a thing,
then I'll take the torch you're carrying
and hurl it backwards so at dawn
all you wake to are empty fields with
nothing left but the charred and bitter embers
of a half remembered plundered past.

The Night After the Assassination

in memory of Julio Fernando Cardona murdered August 7th 2011 Mexico

And I would swallow condoms full
of this star sky and smuggle them home for you
If you'd only tell me where you live now
and if they burst in my intestines
you'll never know
I swallowed stars for you,
that I diced the moon with razors
on the mirror of the sea and sniffed it
past watering eyes to the back caverns of my skull
just to show it to you
on the day of the dead.

The moon can hang there while
I bribe the customs guard
I'll brave the border
with these decorations from a humid night
and the heat I hid in undergarments
and stowed between bare feet and shoes
in the first place they'll think to look
I did it because I want it to be found.

On the day of the dead I'll confess
I looted them
the sky the sea the stars the moon the heat the sweat
I stayed a watch for them
I stayed a watch for you
but I don't know where any of you have gone.

There is another Spain

Four floors up and claustrophobic
just one window facing out, no lift
and suffocating weather pushing
forty degrees in Alicante,
the other side of town
from yachts or sea food restaurants.

Our window, in the kitchen
faced a parallel apartment and
let not one hint of light in,
but you could hear the noise of
our neighbour's incessant shouting;
fighting or lovemaking
but shouting all the same
and before you gave up all thinking
you said it was inspiring how they
could do either in such heat.

And the window in our bedroom
looked down on the shabby coliseum,
a bull ring with faded posters showing
generations of young bullfighters
who walked straight out of Hemingway
every Wednesday afternoon, with girls
in dresses I'd only ever seen in postcards
and brought new words like Gitano,
uneasy, to my tongue.

In the midst of some new breakdown
you clung like a limpet every night
as if I was some secret talisman
but you had never been so distant.

And I knew nothing of apartment living,
nor each evening's macabre killings
or from where the earring wearing gypsies
descended on the town,
and because I had no view on
the listless place you'd gone,
and didn't want one
I looked east from our apartment
beyond the bullring
to the Mediterranean highway
and thought of us two, foolish,
dancing in the kitchen to 'My Girl'
the night that we moved in—
all the way to Barcelona.

Sdrawkcab Allerednic

Intense you said slamming the door
but it could have been worse, if you'd let it
knowing me I'd have given you peripheral vision
for Christmas then a blindfold only I could remove,
from old everyday whims I'd have crafted new limbs
for you to go out on, walked miles on water to save you
if you'd only drown, I'd have shelved my ideals
oh yea, I'd slay them for you, I'd bring back their heads.
Intense you said?

Don't mind those yawning old tropes of spreading
dreams at your feet, me? I'd have spread slicker and faster
than a BP disaster and been harder to clean,
and I'm not talking dreams either—more a plastic bag
to your head I'd have been Ed Munch's worst nightmare
cloying your brain for weeks at a time, like an incessant
Buddy Holly record revolving revolving at 33 rpms
intense you think, me?
Yea, I'm Cinderella backwards.

Hippy Get a Job

You might not realise your predictability but when
you caught my eye on Shop Street at the Demo I could
see the thoughtless words forming in your brain, so before
you shout them at me pass remarkably, let me just
stop you there for once and in the gap between now
and when those thoughtless words make it from your mouth
into the air between us let me tell you something, because
I have wrestled with a pitchfork the same size I was
and shovelled unknown tons of horse manure from sheds
before your mother brought your breakfast toast and tea
on school mornings before your leaving cert.

And when you daydreamed out the window of maths class
from an overheated room into the driving rain, I was
lifting bales of sodden hay through the mud and bitter wind
to the bottom field where the old cow died in spring
and because I had small hands I woke a hundred early mornings
to turn unborn lambs around inside their mothers. While you were
filling college application forms and when you were accepted,
bringing weekend washing home on student discount buses
I was pitting my eight stone against half a ton of pulling racehorse
and couldn't feel my fingers or open my eyes with the rushing wind

You then, qualified and interviewing in your shirt and tie and nerves,
while I was taking sweating tourists on foot through humid rainforests
carrying longhouse chief's heavy gifts of pineapples nine hours back to base
in a country you don't have the breath of mind to even imagine,
and nearer home when you guffawed into your pint glass and refused to leave
Taylor's bar on Sunday early closings I washed your glass, swept the floor
and woke before the county to spend frozen hours putting
rubber bands on live lobster claws in a concrete tank in Bearna

And then I bet you were promoted for your clever corporate antics,
while I did three years mortgage-paying on the night shift
with bleary day time TV addicts and stoners manufacturing,
things you might one day have inserted after too many business lunches
then later on when I decided I needed education and you sat,
with popcorn consuming the latest Hollywood blockbuster
you couldn't see me upstairs splicing your next bit of entertainment.
You have no idea how long a day is invigilating young accountants
in tedium and silence in dusty exam halls with the smell of fast food fat
still clinging to my clothes from my night time cash in hand gig.

You won't realise that I have the streets of Galway imprinted on my brain
from delivering pesto and goats cheese pizza to your Knocknacarra sofa
or that I'm an expert on late night radio, and all night petrol stations
the secondary benefits of an un-free education, and now and here when
I've finally got myself some work I think has merit and I chose to use
this day off, working to defend the rights of others don't be surprised
at all at how quickly I abandon my principles of non-violence and use
this placard on you, as a weapon, if you say what you are thinking.

3am Guest List

I suppose it is that time of night, so welcome in
all you dead and abandoned, please take a seat
on the bed, welcome too ex-es, it's funny I'd been
expecting you'd call, dead dogs and midge bitten
sun-burnt lost days at the lake, this club's not exclusive
why don't you just make yourselves at home in the kitchen
I'll be with you in an instant, uncompleted tasks?
Oh yes we've been introduced, step over this way
with all of the things I said I'd do, but didn't, oh shit
they're here in their numbers, well you'll find
the bathroom is empty, could you all just maybe
perch on the edge of the bath? Unpaid bills—
not you too? Okay then, so be it, you might find at least
that you've much to discuss with my dead aunt in here
on the sofa, she worked in citizen's information and
will make short work of you lot if I'm not mistaken
and yes country music, I do hear you knocking,
and of course I know there isn't a hope you'd miss
a gig like this, but no, no, torch songs, there's no need
for you to perform I had the porch lights left on for just
such an eventuality, be best if you just sit on the floor
here with these legions of melancholy, I don't
really know them that well but they seem to fit in,
and truth, well would you look at what the cat dragged in,
it's typical isn't it, true to form as it were, you're the last one
to arrive and what's more in the morning, you'll be first
out the door and all those delusions and deceptions
who were hanging out here in daylight will refuse
to acknowledge you even exist, oh Christ don't tell me;
that's the doorbell and grim reality says it's on the guest list.

Pooreen Beach Thirty Years On

For Brian

Jesus time passes,
tide's in this time
and it's all here at once,
we left your clear-skinned
children doing what we did
burying each other alive
on the beach, poking fingers
into sea anemones across
lunar-landscape rock pools,
we left our parents
one dozing in a deck chair
one cooking sausages
on a gas stove
and swam out to deep water
at the furthest rock
last stop before Aran
as we used to call it,
or *that way for Boston*
as dad would say
making sure we went
no further, we climbed our
decade barnacled bodies out
onto seaweed strewn rocks
then dived back in
to deep water where
all the currents meet.

Fine day Mrs. Spellman...

I'm from a people bred
for filling empty spaces
with whatever the unspeakable
gap is at the core of us,
but never naming it never
letting on we own it—
but let's not talk about that.

Us two are a mouth making
fierce desolated love
to a lack too altogether new
to grieve for with no teeth,
no voice, no tongue, no lips
and there is no coffin
just the let's-not-talk-about-it
avoidance of any mention
of a corpse.

And I'm resigned to losing
something that never knew
I measured by it, created for it
never knew I loved it but
come on in sit down
and let's not talk about it.

No Man's Land

You know you can seek asylum here,
anytime you want,
on these rain drowned nights
just knock at my front door late on,
I won't overwhelm you with welcomes,
by now we know it takes
a little time for us to readjust
so you can shower, leave wet clothes
drying in the kitchen, I'll make tea
and get you something dry of mine
to wear and we can listen
to late night radio, while we slide
into the old shoes of us,
then sleep together
like inverted commas.

Tomorrow, over breakfast
I'll ask you not to over-think things,
but you'll probably worry at our beads,
that's your way to face for home,
but you know and I do
this no man's land is just that—
it borrows no territory from anyone
and we can seek our shelter here
anytime we want.

Thoughts on you leaving

it's like every basket ball I ever threw
for baying schoolyard onlookers—
missed completely but that's not
saying it, like someone at an ATM
reading insufficient funds three weeks
from payday, but that doesn't cover it
like Norwegians in January craving light
or owls kept up on summer solstice
not knowing what's gone wrong, that's it,
well no something's still missing, maybe
it's more like wishing for the feeling of
curling under a winter-weight quilt to sleep
when it's pushing forty and you're spread-eagled
in the tropics, or like a Minnesota winter freezing
fingers, ear tips, nose, until they're petrifying
now that's close as close as anything but
it's more like coming home on dark streets
late and tipsy to the welcome yellow light
of your own front door but finding nothing
in your pocket when you reach for the key
that instant when you're standing locked out
from your own life it feels a bit like that or like
sitting on a barge front sweeping through fast water
and old rainforest down the Batan-Rajan river
like then I can feel myself diminishing
and it's like that but it's absolutely something different
and for all the far-fetched examples at my disposal
I can't describe how it feels to miss you.

Milking-it

I'm over it please note that,
over stimulated, over elated
over invigorated:
I'm infected, a soft touch
for this lording-over-it cosmos
crowding my brain
with sensations
infiltrating it with people
with places
with full throbbing moons
all ridiculous and un-interpretable.

It's infesting my
thought processes
with feelings it seems all of humanity
must have cast off
and there's no dealing with them,
these legions of orphan emotions
all engaged in a case of mistaken
over identification, I mean it
they're calling me mother
and who is she?
Not me for sure, here
with no milk to give them.

Convention

The guy in the corner enthuses that the chief source of contamination
in any kitchen is from the bin to the counter and vice versa and
he's grimacing knowingly at the waiter's slim hands as they deliver
one more bottle of cheap tranquilizer, an old doll sitting next to him
isn't listening, she's busy explaining that though she isn't religious
she is nonetheless, a very spiritual person, there are a few more laggards
scattered at cheap plastic tables, all bleak looking in the pinks, peaches
and hair bleaches they're doggedly wearing—appropriate by some reckoning
for just such vacations, there's a wind kicking up big time against thin
plastic walls not made for this weather and the waves in their storm force
crashing below us refuse to have anything to do with our cluster of hot air
and bluster in this 'cafe bar' where everything comes with chips and is
accompanied by hits even Elvis wouldn't be seen dead listening to,
an old queen in the corner winks at me and it says hey there sister—
that one's universal, slim pickings his wink says and I'd have to agree,
though I'm not really shopping, but my new found companion across
the table is decrying the state of the current light market he's bemoaning
Chinese resurgence in manufacturing saying, they wouldn't know light
if it hit them in the face and I think the boats below in the harbour
are sparking like a hundred Chinese lanterns but don't mention it
I just watch them while another would-be what he isn't is explaining
that the guy who thought up 'post its' is now worth a fortune but
good fortune like that doesn't strike every day so his motto is to wait
and watch everything or so he tells the Ukrainian who can't follow
a word; you've got to be open, and he's had some successes he says
but it's best not to go into them, not to blow his own trumpet and now
the queen from the corner takes my elbow and whispers you know
from the back I'd my eye on you, but the buttocks were a disappointment
a bit too fleshy, more's the pity and if I had to name my one fantasy
it'd be Michel Angelo's David—he's such a cold bastard but come on
sweetheart, we're leaving, thank god for deviance, and the mini bar
in my room, and I'm with him to the night, to the seafront, arms linking
and we're drinking neither of us giving two fucks for convention.

Flyovers

If there was only one journey,
one road and one manner of walking
I wouldn't mention it but in
this metropolis, this network,
this solar system with all its junctions
and roundabouts all these dizzy orbits
leading us as many directions as
the blue veins running under
the soft white skin on the inside
of your arm, there are options: flyovers
the thing is only to find one,
and when we do, to have the courage
to take it and if I can find it and
you'll come, well I promise I'll take you.

Performance Evaluation

You know it's not as if I need to be employee
of the month and neither praise nor blame
from you will pay my mortgage but if there's
something I'm not doing, or as you choose to put it:
an area you'd like to support me in improving
listen, would you ever give it to me straight?

My time was served where words were tools to
create desired effects and as anyone who's ever
driven cattle somewhere they weren't too keen to go
will get, I'm not talking precision engineering:
wake up you fucking eejit you're about
as much use there as a pair of tits on a bull
would you ever keep your wits about you or
else go in and make the tea...

Or when reversing trailers: Jesus, woman you'd
fit an arctic through what's wrong with you?
If you can't do it get out for fuck's sake and let
someone in who can...
Or that awful day I let five unbroken horses
stampede out a gate I was meant be blocking, listen
no one exactly asked me if there was some way
they could support me in improving.

No; you're nothing but a cunt in boots
is roughly how I recall it and anyway all I'm saying is
would you ever just give it to me straight?
At least then I'll know where I stand
and how to best retaliate.

Arachnophobia

One small brownish common or garden spider unleashed
hysteria in our air-locked hands-washed hairnets
and plastic-socks-over-shoes sterile factory floor
and hysteria, can be seductive and more when it's communal
on the night shift where very little happens.
It was our highest buzz in weeks as eight small legs
in no particular hurry transported a torso that maybe
female spiders would lust over, who knows?

Mick, who spotted it first was notorious for weeks, his stature
unquantifiably increased 'look' he said 'it's a spider!'
and we queued in delicious hysteria to see the little creature
who'd eight legged it in to where he had no business being,
see; our modus operandi, our reason for being was 'a clean room'
yep, that place was clean, and it required senior management
involvement oh I'd say they were chuffed at our diligence
in following their decrees that sterility was to be, the new black.

It took several mid range functionaries trained in crisis management
a few veiled rumours of corporate infiltrators, spying and/or
biological warfare to eke out the max from our high-value hostage
it took focus groups, strategic plans, some key performance indicators,
followed by rigorous evaluation, and not forgetting
one very hard-bitten spider liberation unit (me) who,
taking no prisoners took him to the car park, following
the rule-mandated-general-emergency-site-wide-evacuation
that enabled twenty rooms of captive workers on 10.50 a piece
to toast his freedom over an unscheduled tea break lasting
half an hour; hysterically, I set him free.

Phrase Books Never Equip you for the Answers

on the morning of the fifteenth time we went through
our sleep-with-your-ex routine, I had the usual optimism,
thing about mistakes is to not keep repeating the same ones
I said disregarding the government health warning on
the cigarettes I was sucking, crossing the road without
stopping speaking or looking, ignoring the red man pulsing
on the lights at the junction, I was wired direct, and I said;
I know, I'll write you the definitive user manual for me.
You said I was arrogant that we should make it up as we go
and I said; well could I do a mind map then? With here
be dragons marked clearly in red, so we won't flounder
like last time end up washed up all dehydrated and drained—
well I was fairly wired, I said in each shipwreck we're lessened
embittered, come on, let me at least try to fix it, I can write us
a blueprint for the new improved version, and you laughed
and said well damn you for a head-wreck, go on then and do it.

So I wrote, but it came out all stilted, like a work in translation
see when I say, let me fix that or give it here and I'll do it
it means; I need you, and if I tell you for example, how I'll
re-arrange the universe to your liking it doesn't mean I'm superior
in fact, translated it's about the same as the last one—can you not see
how I need you? And when I come out with all those 'you-shoulds'
that drive you demented, there's no disrespect in 'em, verbatim
they're whispering I'd be desolated without you and when
you call me control freak, the tendencies you're describing are
inherently rooted in my fear of you leaving and how I'll react.
Less-wired more hopeful I brought you my phrase book on
our very next meeting but you kissed my cheek and said let me
stop you a minute and then those awful words that never signify
good outcomes; listen I've been thinking... I know we've got
this weird cyclical attraction thing going and I'm sorry for my part
in it but really I can't see it working, the problem for me is how
you just don't need anything and my phrase book
had nothing listed under that heading.

February's a Hypocrite

Knee deep in mud around a feeder
coat hanger-ed hips, rain scalded spine
doggedly she chews and chews
for warmth alongside vital youngsters
some of whom were calves of hers,
she's hanging on for winter's end.

And Salthill teems with wrapped up people
out in droves to breathe, the first fine evening,
of the first spring night and watch a clear sky
all the way to the lights of Clare
but this February's a hypocrite
and old cows die in March.

Nods and Winks

(*AI—Artificial Insemination)

There wasn't a wild amount of hedonism abroad then in Ennis mart
just the usual doses of steamed windows, mashed spuds
of limp cabbage philosophies, hanging out from tweed caps
of winter noses, and the odd imperceptible nod to himself in the ring
adding gravy to proceedings, and the thing with nods is
the less obvious the bigger the spectacle, and our home grown
life theories echoed round by the manure reeking butcher's dozen;
it's burying old cows when it's the same hole in the ground we'll
end up in, there's no living to be had in farming this weather
without tweaking the system, it's the same hole you'll end up in,
pushing up daisies, no use killing yourself is there? For the department
or the travelling AI man who'd fleece you as quick as he'd
look at you, flashing his pictures of Belgian Blue bulls in
summer pastures as if they were holiday brochures and the joke
of how he was both producing and selling, was as near to humour
a farmer could get to when drab days in February that'd freeze
the bollix off you are repeating like jokes told over and over when
there are no walls worth a fuck against the wind in February
and the best of dry land's so like a swamp underfoot it'd pull
the boots off you and in Ennis the only warm taint of a scandal
was the odd rumour of cattle tags being changed, and we all knew
who'd do it and had used him but didn't let on though we'd repeat it
to be saying, something, in February oh there'll be trouble and plenty
and we all got warm affirming how much plenty there would be,
to each other's pinched faces, and some said it was the wipers
not working, or the wet road and the bend those fuckers in the council
hadn't marked out though we were near mute from telling them
and still more said they'd told him that car heater would kill him,
sure they'd poleaxe anyone after a day spent in the cold, and
the trouble on-coming we'd spent weeks discussing was only hinted at,
then only in passing, the conclusion agreed was that he nodded off
at the wheel, could happen to anyone and no one would say
that a one-car collision, not a drop of drink in him, well, no one
entertained that his fatality was anything but chance, for fear
we'd catch it ourselves some evening out, counting sheep,
worth nothing, in a never ending winter.

Dear John / Jane

If you want the truth whatever that is we met when
I was bored, and if you must know I've never found
pierced nipples that attractive anyhow, yours in particular
played havoc with my fillings spoiling an otherwise
exemplary performance with unbecoming winces,
in fact I could hardly ever bear to touch you but it wasn't
as if a queue had formed awaiting my attention and you
were best of the scant few lined up for the slaughter
but yes, you're right there was some genuine affection
mostly mine for me, and you were quite obliging supplying
applause where there should have been none and now
you're here insisting that I owe you some 'closure'
Jesus, there's one delusion with a lot to answer for,
so as ordered, coming up the truth served cold is that
I didn't give a fuck and don't I was only going
through the motions. Dear John or Jane or whatever
you said your name was, I didn't love you. I was bored.
Yours fondly,
In closure.

John the Shirt

for John the shirt

I remember when we were
a double act
the uncrowned king and queen
of Cuba night club
of coffee shops, new-fangled Cappuccinos
of trips in convoy to concerts dodging cops
of Freddie White singing Desperados
of breaking hearts, our infamous double act
seductions where despite our swagger
we nearly always came off worst
then consoled each other—
sure fuck it she's not worth it;
we weren't usually that bothered,
and in Amsterdam's red light you
were an exuberant bright shirt Casanova
until you saw the first window
with a woman in it
and got disgusted, sickened
you said Sarah that could be
my sister and I loved you for it—
who wouldn't? And of the forty different jobs
I had across continents while you
clocked in the same one since school
and damn proud of it,
but you drove me to the airport
waved me off, and of changes,
unavoidable adjustments
that meant after two decades
as gun slinging compadres we drifted
and at your father's funeral I walked
behind your badger-grey hair
and grieving shoulders
watched you shepherd your young family

behind the man you could never please,
but always tried to
and I thought, good men are scarce
but you always know them
when you see them.

Blame Walt Whitman

I should never have brought you to sit on these dunes in all their
kitsch holiday bleakness, I know this is a place that hurts you but
at least you know it, and I should have refused to take you down
streets looking for the Santa Muerte when those were my own
dark journeys, or to the port in the evening where things feel
different, nothing there is female but maybe that's what I wanted
to show you, I can't believe I took you to look at children's corpses
when it's my buzz to name the dead and most days I know it has
less purpose than scrawling 'I was here' on the brutal walls that
will outlast me, and you with that conflicted DNA hardwired
your essence would be to sharp-tongue it, you'd call it an experiment
in detachment to touch those baseball caps and soiled jean legs
with my own fingers and not in turn be touched and I can hear
you say; will that be your epitaph Sarah, nothing touches you?
But I know in our connection you've only got more gentle words
for me no matter if I've never earned them, and in fairness you were
with me when I sat and watched white-lime letters spelling 'Tito'
carved out on a sickly green hill in a country so pastoral you could
see why violence just might be the antidote, maybe anything is better
than triteness? And putting my hands in sun-warmed war-damaged
pock marks on sandstone buildings in that split city Mostar, you called
it escapism and shook your head but you wrapped two arms
around me from behind from across those misnomer peace walls
that are your geography and I wanted you to do it —that means
something, doesn't it, even if it's only back ground music?
Or that day I showed you the Lipizzaner horses and you said nothing
but I knew you were thinking what has she got against comfort
and so I said I know with all the things I've done, this might sound
like hypocrisy but if I had my way I'd set them all free and in
the fakeness of bad wine and literary conversations later, you said
there's not one true thing here and winked that if you'd your way
you'd set them all free and let freedom be their new poetry and I
guess its faith of some kind when you never ever asked to be
brought with me to places I hadn't any need to go but I took you

to the Cafe de la Habana where you told me to go a bit easier
on myself and it's funny how I couldn't bring myself to listen
even though I wanted to hear it, so I went down Avenida Reforma
and dragged back the young man you were curious about and I
fucked him on the floor for you because you were curious and
because it was easier than hearing him say so much nothing
and it cost me very little except the sound of a downpour that would
have been better heard alone and if I said what I remembered
of our encounter it'd be the drone of one persistent mosquito who
might or might not have been responsible for the purple bruises
on my neck that made me think of you after, and I did it as a way
to break your dead grip on having said forever and discovering
you'd never meant it and sometimes physicality is easier than
to listen to you talking, I don't know if it was vicarious when I couldn't
be bothered reporting how the evening light caught on his alabaster
haunches and how so alone you can be when you don't feel anything
except the ebb and flow of pulses and I know you'll get me when I
say for that one it's fair to blame Walt Whitman and you came with me
to where the glass shatter sirens and songs of revolution choked you,
those lines of union workers singing The Internationale in the dead heat
of a random Sunday in two thousand and eleven? When they
clench fisted in unison you whispered that you couldn't see anything
true in it and I said so let's set them all free you and me and on
the strength of it I bought you those carved out imaginary animals
from a street child but then I never sent them because in all the things
dissolving that I was certain of, I was unsure of their welcome
and in New York we all absconded down through streetscapes so
familiar that it felt like trying to swallow something when my mouth
was empty maybe trying to swallow the idea that me the unbeliever
the heretic believes that you've been with me all this time and in
all these places on the strength of one slim every day connection.

Dog Days

I keep my hood up
on wet streets
and a weather eye out,
ready to skirt down
a side-road should I see
someone familiar.
I half-see miniatures,
backs of heads
in front of TV screens
in time-warp ground floor
apartments, where I've no
business being.

Along the dim path
by the river swans
puff their defences
my way though
their cold hearts
aren't in it, nor mine either
if it comes to it,
I pass your street-level
lit window evenly going,
eyes on the pavement,
half-wishing someone
would commit me,
take it out of my hands.

A stray dog tags
for a couple of metres,
then gives up, thinking
the better of fixing his fortunes
to mine I'm half-grateful,
half-sorry, it's no exaggeration
to say that his warm tongue

on my hand could
have swamped me
because tonight
even one small kindness
would be an undoing.

Days With a Dog in Them

When you wake in the humour
to bark at the postman yourself
when your jeans won't stay up
and though your breakfast sticks
itself to the front of your shirt
the mirror in the bathroom neglects
to say anything about it and you
only find out when you're called
to a 'you must try harder in future'
haranguing from your boss, when
you try to ring a taxi as a last ditch
attempt to compensate for your lateness
and find you've a tub of margarine
in your bag which means your phone
is probably chilling at home on the shelf
of the fridge, when you're at the wrong angle
to everything with footpaths conspiring
to tilt away from your feet and you'd have
more chance of landing a space ship
than parallel parking your car
when every conversation is an
argument gestating and you're a mess
of nerve endings of itches and glitches
and trigger fingers that can't wait
to shoot but you haven't the foggiest
what it is you're so determined to kill
these are the days when you need
some old mongrel on duty to grin
you hello from its half rotten teeth
and cavort its old bones in dances
of stiff legged welcome while you
set about barricading the world out
of your house, as some old fella told me;
there's no use is there, in buying a dog
then doing all the barking yourself?

Old Dog Old Tricks

I've often been told that the male
of the species is never too old
and I have a hold of your arm
so we can cross the rush hour road
and you know it, don't you?
You're like an old dog strutting
on the tips of his toes with grey ears
alert, joints creaking and
you proffer a hopeless exposure
a baring of washed-up charm
nothing concrete now, not even
a look you or I could explain;
we're talking a flicker here a knowing
I know it, and you do, it's us two
in a different dimension,
a different relation to living
a shape shifting where fifty years
could mean nothing, somewhere
there's a warp, an aspect where
we could have been something
and in the hotel lobby I find you a seat,
order tea, pass you a napkin, and we
pass a grey evening leaving
everything rueful unspoken.

Grief Three Months On

You meet it
corridors of it
gone is gone
and totally unlike
the colourful fear of losing
with its waterfalls of hurt.
This now, a barren moonscape
a grey institutional corridor and
you must walk it like the damned.

I Flick Channels While...

Ana drives two Guatamalteca girls from Tapachula
to the border, steering them clear of mass-graves and countless
faceless rapes, if she doesn't text me every hour 'til
they reach Puebla she asked could I ever ring her father
in the capital, Desperate Housewives is nearly over and
it's the ads, as Louise from school gets small patches
of her hair shaved off by a nurse working nightshift,
tomorrow while I eat breakfast and read the paper
they will shock her brain with static. She went on a bus
to the cliffs of Moher last week the same wet night we
drank wine in Nimmos remembering Blondie lyrics together
and we all say this is better. Christ what would we know?
But we hope. Jose in Cork toasts Che's anniversary
then downs one for Castro in the damp asylum seeker's hostel.
He's got a cube, a box room he shares with three men
from countries at war with each other over something
and the Irish weather has him wheezing but he says the government
is giving them their own apartments shortly, that's the refugee
bush telegraph working overtime and I won't contradict it.
A slim chance is better than not any, isn't it? Tonight while
the news is spouting financial crisis Irish people are finding
sea legs and swallowing acid nerves when they could have
stayed home to watch The Week in Politics but they're sailing
for Gaza where Khaled's children have never seen a cinema
or taken a train journey and they could do nothing but
a slim chance is better isn't it, than not any? And hope sails
on all types of winds and storm fronts doesn't it?
Well here's hoping, anyway.

Past Tense

I know that look you woke with
some jaded has-been day before
is still plucking at your clothes,
queasy over breakfast, weren't you?
Yesterday's cornflakes leaden
in your gut, and behind your shower curtain
songs sung to scare the dark
were warbled little hands clenched in
someone else's pockets, someplace
you don't remember being
but know you were.

Make no mistake the past
is this same place and like it or whatever
we're permanent inhabitants,
on shifting tectonic plates sits
the playground loner; twelve,
strapped in your rear seat a stalwart of ten,
the driver a hysteric, a heretic of the future;
she knows only this and that exist.

And I live for eons in the half light
of eight's imaginings of nothing like this
still not fluent in these twisting tenses
fluxing 'whens' conditionals; if I'd only
well only what? I can no more
tell you at thirty-one or at half past
five tomorrow than you could listen
in the instant, take though,
take this illusion I've built you
and hold it. It keeps me here.

Un-learning

Lately I've been erasing how the first time I touched
one uncertain finger to your neck would feel and it's taken
a lot of walking a few nights wine drinking and one or two
re-visits to old gentle ghosts still breathing and forgiving.
I've rubbed out every terse involuntary shiver you would
have ever given and especially I've deleted all traces of where
I didn't press my lips against your collar bone, your wrists.
I've annihilated all anticipatory sensations from my stomach
those preludes to nothing that stemmed from knowing exactly
how I'd please you without losing anything, now it's a silent
graveyard filled with lumpen butterfly corpses though
the patient remains stable. Doesn't she always? I've talked
an awful lot of waffle to people who were unwitting accomplices
in this rewriting of an entirely one dimensional longing.
I've been pretty busy unlearning how it would feel for us
to sleep there, wake there and to remember both forever and now
I expect you to play your part and take that duster to the dust motes
of this farce, I mean on the scale of unrequited is that so very much
to ask? Do this for me? Unlearn us.

Warning for Dreamers

There's a lot to be said
for holding tightly to bleak
outlooks, there's comfort
in them and a style about it,
it's affirming facing up to simple
predictable grimness, go on admit it:
there's a dogged old ease to it,
keep a close watch though
on those imps of wisps of dreams
who'll grow like weeds in cracks
where it seems they've nothing
to live from or for, and hope,
when you least expect it
when you've already envisaged
the worst possible projections,
and declared yourself equal to them,
well hope will bowl in uninvited
and derail you in an instant if
you don't keep an eye on it.

Indictment

An amorphous cluster high jinks it
through Gardiner Street's
November grime, teenage hands
grasp lurid cans of some toxic
energy elixir, the slim frontrunner,
has a dancer's waist, and her over
lip-glossed mouth spews words fit
for a docker, blaggarding all
and sundry, it's innocence of some
sort or other that the worst invectives
they can think of are faggot, loser, dickhead
and she's swanking, flaunting a too-brief
flush of freshness that has her
crew-cut white-socks and runners posse
bobbing after, gangly ankley cowboys
to a man, in year or two she'll be
skanger, haggard and her band
of merry outriders will have conveniently
wizened so we don't see them swept
in corners. You and I will think it 'Skanger'
before our better nature politically corrects us
on Lower Abbey Street they pass the theatre
with its intelligentsia queuing.
Culture? This is Ireland, welcome
and have you met our children?

This Particular Much Always Wants Less

Just now the look you gave me,
while I was changing was a cue,
a prompt from the wings, it said
time's up pack your bags
get your things,

it was like that voice
from a train's intercom system
enticing incessantly alight here,
alight here...and I will,

what am I on about?
You might well ask, it's like this see;
I'd rather send you postcards
or tell strangers about you,
when I'm drunk and melancholic
in far-off bars, and for the record
the seedier the better,

I'd eat those nuclear-packed
airplane lunches or take a pack
and a stick and think walking
how I miss you, while I
burn off the damned leeches,

I'd watch martial-arts movies
on air-conditioned buses in Asia,
I'd travel in pickups
with wood planks for seats,
and inhale the same air as
tubercular babies
being carried in slings,

I'd prop my feet on sacks
of some produce that turns out
to be maggots,
turns my stomach and
I for one won't be eating them,

so I'll just stare out the back window
as the past disappears on some dirt road
behind me and I'll miss it, ·
I can't wait till I'm missing it,

listen I know there's more
than one way to skin it,
but this is my story
and you've got your lines in it
I could I suppose have warned
you they were pre-scripted
and you've only the one
which is; goodbye, see you later
or if you're not overly bitter
travel safe, which I will

but it helps to have someone
I need to shake off
and the glimpse of our slippers
and sofas and dotage
in your last look
was reason enough to board
whatever form of transport
is nearest so I can think
of our lost future
without you interrupting,

yep, I know there are more
ways to skin it but I do mine
like this; this particular much
always wants less.

Disappearances can be Deceptive

In memory of Mariano Abarca, RIP 2009, Chiapas, Mexico

At ten past six here
you'll be able to mourn
the disappearance of the tropical sun
that baked your hairline
at ten to,
two hundred whole languages
have vanished
and the people who objected are
invisible
washing windscreens
at city junctions.

The virgin of Guadalupe though
appeared
as if from nowhere in 1531
and 1910 had every appearance
of a revolution
but Blackfire Exploration can show up
from Canada
to atomise a mountain and its villages
in six months and though
there is no apparent
department for state disappearances
Mariano Abarca
who resisted
disappeared,
no one saw anything
and the raped virgin soil said:
nothing.

Is There not Someone Else you Could Call?

On the occasion
of the seventh rescue
in one month and on a day
when I have been
asked advice on bleeding boilers
press releases,
how to draw welfare
emigration legislation,
asked to lend out a projector
and a fourteen mm spanner
for a loan of my passport
by a disorganized traveller
I've donated three cigarettes
one tenner and
have four friends looking
to sleep on one sofa
can I draw this
small request to your attention:

next time,
your car breaks down
in torrents of rain
and you haven't got a jack
maybe, would you
could you,
scroll down the contacts
on your phone
a little past C
for Clancy? There are
twenty five other letters
if you're working in English,
and a few more to play with
in most other languages
and Jacks?
There's a reason
people have them.

Could you possibly,
next time he has cheated
and you need to explain
how you'd no idea
this tenth time
that he'd even wandered
tell it to someone
who hasn't heard it before
and made the decision to
be single?

And when you think
your teenager is doing drugs
please don't make me
the expert, remember
I have no children,
or I promise to introduce
them immediately
to my dealer
who is the king of all
sleazes.

And if you feel you're
having one more breakdown
please don't ask me
to take the ferry
to your country
to dispense support
and be dispensed with
shortly after
or I will turn tables
and take up residence
on your sofa
and I guarantee you
I will howl
on your shoulder
at any slight
provocation
and for an interminable
duration.

Sleeping Dogs and Half Truths

Incandescent, I'll use that language,
it's in the vernacular for sure for our
most extravagantly husbanded lie.
I miss it and the way we cultivated it
tended to it, gravitated round it
in evangelistic embrace, in orbit we were
bill-boarding it in tasteless neon, savouring
the resultant spectacle's sheer patina of veracity,
more flavourful by far than any old banal pursuit
of accuracy and what of it if we drank deep,
swallowed and half believed?

We acclimatised to it you and me;
measured exteriors lengths and breadths by it
adapted to its altitude, we evolved, grew feet
and walked on land with it, described emperor's
rig-outs while the poor bastards shivered but
we didn't concern ourselves at all with goose-pimples
just fleshed it out and made it corpulent, until
the day you went and asked me what I really thought;
you made a wizened, devastated myth of it.

Shhh...

La Muerte Tiene Permiso

I read a book once about an African with aids, in it the narrator
asked a sympathizer will you not die too white man? Now,
with us two lying here at the edge of sleep you want me to
analyse my formative experiences—please! I want something too;
I want you to sleep, I can say I'm glad and mean it, more even
I mean I'm suffused in this present with you in it but you want me
to embark on excavating my past when any start point would be
as arbitrary as dead stars in their millions, listen there is no beginning.
Can I not just stare at reflections without itemizing which of your ribs
protrudes since the famine, which since Adam? Do you need me to
spell out how the words I think in are a language donated,
unasked for? I know if I object to discussion you'll say it helps to talk
and it's a point alright but I don't remember conceding that any help
was needed. Listen; where I live Lorca's still walking and each
pavement we're using is built on dead-heads, but here I am
with you in our atheist's prayer to existence, and the dead are here too
flesh in our grasp—our past has no meaning when it's here and
it's breathing when layers and layers of death and I are talking,
sleeping and dreaming and we're in love with your fingers on our
collarbones and twisted in our hair. Before you spoke I was thinking
along lines of thanksgiving because we're together I was wearing it
lightly, and by asking you've made me wonder if what I sensed
as perfect and current has some emotion missing, thanks, thanks
for asking. I read a book about an African with aids where he asked
his sympathiser will you not die white man? And you will you not
die with a collection of senses assaulted by despair by devotion
by humour, by boredom or tortured by sunsets so perfect they left
scars on your soul, on the souls of the dead and the blank souls
of the living as if there is, or was, any difference? Will you not die
in a surfeit of reactions piled up like layers of old rock? Call me
a pop psychology failure if you have to but don't ask me to decipher
which aspects of me I can attribute to this that or the other, listen;
I haven't a notion but I'm sure of one thing, I'll die too, death as

they say in Mexico, has permission and when it does when I let it breathe in the everyday, match my steps when I'm walking then everything still living has permission to flourish, like fear-growing, desperation and this warm nest of our devotion to breath taking-do something for me? Shhh, just listen we're saying it by breathing.

The Most Bombed Place on Earth

For Martin Sharry

In Luang Prabang the lonely-planets float
in inner tubes down the same Mekong
the Pol Pot swimmers and Viet Cong did
before arriving in the birthplace of Bob Dylan
and in the twin cities Martin sang The Fields
to Laotian Karaoke and we ate sticky rice
at the Asian buffet with those we were displacing,
who loaded platefuls as if in fear of famine and
prison labour sandbagged the bursting Mississippi
while we drove their jobs to Boston Airport.
In Vientiane American tourists laughed
over French coffee at the concrete factory picture
on the currency and locals steered them clear
of the land the amputee we met in Louisburg
hadn't got around to de-mining.

What I Forgot is...

In memory of Sergio Contla, RIP, December 2011

that in Oaxaca Zocalo the adolescent shoe cleaners,
just-past toddler trinket-sellers and the shoeless
singing guitar player are philosophers and
drop-everything pigeon-chasers who laugh as much
as I do. The San Juan Copala women sleeping
underneath the arches of a thousand tourist feet
can't go home from the corner they've camped in
since nearly this time last year so they stay here
like installations outside the museum of modern art.
The government in all its generosity has provided
porta-loos as a symbol of how much they like democracy
and sure why wouldn't they? But they say nothing
of the tail that's wagging them or how the house
that jack-boots built and armed is now held hostage
by Paramilitary kids all busy killing women who
are not too terribly concerned with the arrangements
for their defecation and the waiters there to serve us
in the haunts of people seeking Paz and Carlos Fuentes,
or any other trinket of a real Latino junket are not
too easily fooled either. You and me? They've seen us
and they know when we've had our fill of Mayan ruins
and Tequila we'll just leave them on our plates with our
stubbed out cigarettes and practiced Spanish phrases
and we'll think no more of them than the fifty pesos we
tossed behind us as we left—that's the currency we trade in.

Things you put on the net

for Alli

Sleepless at four AM and feeling raw
as chewed skin at the edge of a fingernail,
flicking through junk mail that advised extending
my credit, shrinking my waistline or trusted friend
I've inherited money and I heard you could help—
when I found, ten year old messages from you,

telling me you felt weightless by the Berlin wall
your antipodean airiness perplexing both Germanys,
saying, you knew that you missed me but
wasn't it strange how we were better apart
than squeezing these egos together,
misquoting, you wrote Mario Benedetti said
the miracle was that a-swim in this vast sea
of people, us two met, and we did, but that wasn't
Benedetti, and yes, I know how you hate to be wrong,
but you'd signed all the mails with
soul sunshine, and the kind of hug
that makes your eyes water

I thought, how harshly I'd rewritten you,
how in hindsight, scars are just so much calloused skin,
and ten years late, I wrote you a mail to say
I also remember, how you'd curse me for
my stubborn work ethic
from the shipwreck of our bed,
but you'd still send me off every morning
with kisses fit for a sailor
at the end of shore leave, how
breakfast and lunch were a riot of pots
and really you were never that tidy,
but now I'm no longer sure if it matters,
I know, there's a slim to none chance you'll get it,
I accept there's been a torrent under our bridge,
but you know, anything put on the internet
floats out there forever.

Ringing in Sick to go Mermaid Hunting

Once when I wasn't, I called in sick for the evening shift
and went instead to meet you at Raftery's in Kilcolgan,
so we left your car there and I drove south-west
down the summer solstice evening, hitting for the coast
we squinted through sunglasses at Ballinderreen and Kinvara
but didn't stop, turned for Fanore at Ballyvaughan, you leaning back
feet on the dash singing along to the Indigo Girls and Johnny Cash,
asking me where we were headed, but messing about,
I wouldn't say, I told you on a day like this, trust me
it will all work out: we're going mermaid hunting
and the signs are good for catching.

There were no mermaids though, at the pier before Blackhead
just one dolphin doing her bit for inter-speciel integration
she came in waist-deep to meet us and we were charmed,
and drenched. From behind wet hair you asked me how
I'd known and in my stupid humour I said oh you know
I had my people call her people, that's how it goes,
this event was arranged for your pleasure dear.

You pushed me backwards off the pier then jumped
yourself and our dolphin circled as if she got the joke,
spearing herself four feet skywards above our heads
then vanishing beneath. Us two fools, we swam through seaweed,
feeling elemental and amateur, you're half fish you said,
yea but I've caught you this time.

In Lenane's at dusk we had chowder, and a pint,
I sat with salty skin and hair and when you joined
the jobs-worth band to sing 'The Dimming of the Day' for me,
you made every hair on every sunburned neck there stand.
You slept then as I drove but I woke you in Kilcolgan to send you
down the Craughwell road, me? I hit for home, but parked
instead at Whitestrand beach, on the longest evening of the year
too full of everything to go inside just then.

Sad Bear's Dance

In the middle of a critique of post-feminist lit the academico asked for
examples, she cased the joint for samples. You there in the corner
she pointed, how do you identify? And like I do when put on the spot
I back-answered, retorted, as chat ups go, sweetheart that one's a
keeper, and I'm really liking the cut of your jib. She insisted excitedly
that I was manifesting a particularly insidious strain of patriarchy and
said sisters and the few selected males amongst us, do you see how
our specimen is acting unwittingly contrary to feminist interests?
Seems she's internalised, oh yes she's aping it, so picking fleas from
my pelt I said well in the interests of political correctness are we
talking here gender or sex? And she: whichever, I'm asking are you
an X or a Y and if you're happy with that designation or do you feel
you've been put in a box? Never till now I was thinking but she just
wouldn't be stopped: I'm asking did you learn it or just be it,
chromosomally speaking, science we're talking, not myth? So I said
ahh, science is it? Why didn't you say? Well you'll be happy to know
I'm empirical, a walking experiment and I propose that there are
waaaaay more letters than that. I'm a boy if you want, a man for all
seasons but when the moon calls I'm her bitch, I'm a wave that never
comes far enough in, an eight year old child in a dress, in my father's
high heels call me princess and while we're at it get down on your
knees for your king, sure if we're talking here subject and object
then I'm the rent boy you've always wanted to bugger I'm a work
in progress—might never be finished, a construction fallen foul of
the bust. I'm rubble, fictitious, making it up as I go now gender all those
if you wish. Because when the whim takes me I'll be a welder in denim
I'll sing soprano without a note in my head, I'm a trickster, orator,
a mother, a mute, I'm a no-good mechanic, times are I'm ex-rated,
a eunuch frustrated, back at you there sweetheart tell me, who is it
that wants to know? I'm a name on your label; Mammal, Amphibian,
Fish out of Water. I'm a sexless conquestless Casanova, an afterthought
studied to within an inch of my life, a Petri dish, a sea horse, ambidextrous
all at once left centre and right, sure fuck it why stop there while we're
at it, let's abstract it; I'm an insomniac owl at your window banging

the pane with my beak, I'm a wheat field well sometimes I am it, then
sometimes I'm in it, sometimes perversely I'm sand. Today I'm a cowgirl
in leather and I'm cracking this whip for the kicks, tomorrow I could have
my legs crossed, perfume reeking from each of my wrists, so come on in
with your cork board and microscope, sure I'll prostrate myself for your pin,
why wouldn't I? When I'm my own favourite blank canvas an artwork
unfinished and I'm thoroughly glad of your interest. Here listen, yea I know,
eureka! we could begin our own travelling freak show and go out on
the road if you wish, we'll meander through small towns and hamlets
and nothing and when the crowds gather I'll get my kit off, I'll strip to entice
them while you pocket our ill-gotten loot, then later when it's quiet and
they've gone I'll slow dance on your chain like the saddest of bears until
someday when I'll about face and savage you in that way no one ever
predicts, however often this rictus of captive and victor's enacted, and
I'll be happy at it let me tell you, happy as a striped jacketed monkey
transplanted to the coldest of streets, I'm a one trick pony reading up on
peripheral vision, realising I have it and asserting that I can grind
any organ I wish and I trust that answers it.

Cave Paintings

From down here on Fanore beach in early spring
(*dog walkers, couples and hardy surfers*)
the bleak small Burren hills appear dramatic
like some imposing Afghan mountain range
and cattle perched on their stone faces
have as little form as cave paintings
and the brown wooden bridge on the dunes
from the chipped and forlorn campsite,
(*barbecues mobile homes and Bearna huts*)
is as out of place as the bridge back to you
I can't seem to burn.

Carried Away

We whiled away words there
in the warmth, in dim light
in the mischief of afternoon drinking
and we drank with abandon
as if we could afford it and laughed
as though nothing was serious
in daylight drinking there are no befores,
no afters, so we drank and half heard
songs seeping and paid neither heed
nor attention to hard chairs,
to Spanish hams hanging
or to the aimless waiters who knew us
and took no notice, lost in their own
after lunch lull, that hour when
secrets are so easily shared except
that us two had no need for soul baring;
there deep in the hold of Friday's
mid-afternoon where nothing has gravity
we floated, confessed nothing to no one
and look where it got us.

Bertin, Alejandro and Rogelio

In memory of Bertin, Alejandro & Rogelio,
killed on the 31st Oct 2009 in Guerrero, Mexico

There's a chalked out hopscotch
on a tree-lined street
beside the high stone wall
that cradles Trotsky's house
and it's hard to picture violence here

The uniformed guard dozes
a radio playing at his side
and the summer music carries
onto a silent dappled street
and it's hard to picture violence here

In the park grey and black squirrels
devour nuts from tiny children's hands
while smiling parents watch,
then dart, ungrateful, up the trees
you couldn't imagine violence here

At the Cuyoacan market
twin tiny yellow birds sing out,
with not a wingspan's space
in their gaudy painted cage
and you couldn't imagine violence here

Last Saturday troops in a Humvee
killed three Guerrero boys
of no more than seventeen
in 1940 Trotsky lost his life here
and there's no hint of violence to be seen.

Revolt

for Tadhg McGrath

When the dust has settled
I'll be put to death with the well fed
that's the way it is and I'm not sorry.

At the barricade brute truth is in the bullets, not the Molotovs.
At the ballot the answers are in the batons sheathed, not the boxes.
On the marches the purpose is the provocateurs not the speeches.

The point is not causing conflict or trouble-making
it's about forcing the gate keepers to expose the real rules
of this game we're entrapped in.

It's about displaying who calls the shots, who fires them
and who feels them.

Resilience

Though I sat on the knees of Redemptorists
and Jesuits, served a few Sundays at mass
and hung around bishop's palaces
no priest ever asked me. In truth
if they had I would've probably
assented like I did for the collarless
all gathered now baying for this new reformation
but it takes a whole village to rape a child
and at eleven when I heard of the missions
my first thought was to join them but later
it dawned that that too is rape, there is no escaping
and to date we've built no system that isn't.

At the Truth and Reconciliation, the man
who'd lost his old Mercedes to the conflict
seemed more damaged than a boy of twelve
who'd dismembered his own mother at gunpoint.
But who is it anyway that gets to say if it's a crime
to be resilient under trees grown tall with bloodshed?

I could describe the iconic bullet ridden
location this happened at,
could go into how this country's people
ripped one another to shreds in a conflict
as reason, as rhyme-less as any,
but all I'll say is that day, in hot sunshine
an old man, skin brown from exposure,
swam by a bridge, in a fast flowing river,
and you can decide if it was
Mostar,
Letterfrack,
Belfast,

Palestine,
Congo
Liberia,
Tibet,
Iraq,
Sudan
or Afghanistan, no matter,
all I'm saying is:
people swim,
after.

No Triumphalism

If I have to I will nail your coffin shut myself.
Gravely, don't worry you can't cringe from there,
so gravely, I'll throw a first poignant fistful of clay on
its wooden lid, then shovel until I can hear the dense
imprecise sound of earth hitting earth. I'll do no
dance steps on it, no, nothing so tasteless, I'll just
spread the lurid faux-grass mat over it and walk.

Observers, if there are any will more than likely report
that I went about my tasks calmly, practically and
with respect, and they might even be correct, as yet
I have no way of knowing how those emotions will sit
what I can say though is, as sure as death and taxes
I will walk from the cemetery with a chapter closed
and its lid shut tightly even, if I have to do it myself.

No Bells or Whistles

I can't isolate the precise moment
of surrender other than to say
it was roughly mid-morning
and I succumbed for no good
or conscious reason, certainly
it wasn't the wintery light washing
the life from your features
and we weren't, by a long shot
in the most romantic of settings
but I was sitting with cold hands
clenched in my pockets, sweatshirt
zipped to the neck, chin tucked in,
with a coiled-spring chill playing
on my over-caffeinated nerves
and hunching my shoulders
then you laughed, and there was
something ever so real in it,
and that was me gone,
it's not easy at this age to muster
the optimism to think this
will go anywhere, no, there'll be no bells,
no whistles, more likely it'll be grist
for insomnia-powered mills
but what the hell the dream
and the dreamed don't wait for permission
and it's landed, you're lovely, I'm lost
and there's no use in resisting.

KindlyCompleteyourPurchasesandProceedtothe NearestCheckoutImmediatelythisStoreisnowClosing

A particular way of speaking got lodged in my sphincter; we'll call it
a cliché affliction for a whole wet month it stuck like too sweet cake
and every time I spoke, out the fuckers came; it could happen a
bishop, great day for ducks and we are where we are god help us,
then the dog ones started; his bark is worse than his bite, old dog
for the hard road, every dog has his day, let sleeping dogs lie—
the tail was wagging this dog alright and I said them all in response
to totally unrelated questions, thinking I may as well be hung
for a sheep as a lamb, I made hay while the sun shone—in January
no less and I told every early bird I spotted they'd worms
for catching, I mean it, get the name of an early riser and you can
sleep all day I said to narcoleptics, I told the dozy bastards that if
it wasn't for bad luck—they wouldn't have any, but there's no road
without a turn in it I said, act in haste repent at leisure, I said them,
out they came, the fuckers and I couldn't stop, I was like everyone
you never wanted to listen to assembled together for your pleasure.
The following month as if in some cosmic trick or other I started with
the quotes, Oscar of course, both the Wilde and Muppet Show versions
Ghandi too, be the change! I told anyone who'd listen, I went black
then—Mandela, Martin Luther and The Panthers—against the wall
motherfucker, I told the doctor and I even spouted Malcom X and
called my local representative a house Negro of which he was fairly
undeserving being white as snow that's never been pissed on, all
you have to lose is your chains I told the Mayor and predicted he'd
lose them, oh well easy come easy go I said with wisdom and then
the worst month by far kicked off when all I could say were phrases
from supermarkets that I didn't even know I remembered—I told
the man at welfare that there was better value in our fruit and veg
department and he said I was a nutter. Customers, I told him,
kindly complete your purchases and proceed to the nearest checkout
immediately this store is now closing and as they dragged me out
the door I thought I wanted my own voice back to decide what to say
when I'd say it and so I took a vow of silence—for those who know me

you'll know I wouldn't find that easy and the minute I shut up I heard
two birds singing, no, no I did, and I said to myself an empty vessel
makes most noise and realised I'd landed back at go with clichés
flowing and I thought I was unique—a precious specimen until
the car park attendant said there's your ticket love and remember
no Viet Cong ever called me nigger then the guy in the cafe said
there wasn't any use in crying over spilt milk as he spilled it—crying,
I told my therapist and she was no better she said; sweetheart
sure these things happen.

Out of its misery

There are so many sweet poems
about blackbirds and now this one
who isn't really black is baleful,
grounded, blameful and me,
who threw rasher rinds
on the pathway for a timid faint-heart
cat, all fur and nails and slink:
now I'm chief executioner
reporting for duty and the tiny bird
is flightless more feathers strewn
than any creature this size could need,
its beak brandished my direction
in open orange defiance is
as flamboyant as lipstick
on an old folk's ward where all
is beige and white and I'm here
steel shovel raised to do the needful
but the worst thing is that I know
I have it in me.

I Crept Out

It was half past eleven on a weeknight you were sleeping
and I thought the day was far from over but I felt it wouldn't
have much purpose however much I stretched it if the extra hours
I wrung out didn't involve you so I kissed your eyelids
then crept out in soft shoes and I stole this white-legged horse
for you. It wasn't easy and ever since his restless tail's been
flicking at the wet recesses of my eyes so you keep asking
if I'm crying but I can't answer because I always have to creep off
to distract him from his incessant foot stamping, in case you hear it
and while you watched the evening news I crept out to feed him
the spoils from our small kitchen. I gave him grapes and seeds
and oat flakes from my palm and I sang our song to calm him
while he was eating and I've been busy muffling up his snortings
with fake coughs—I've had to take up smoking so you don't hear him
blowing and suspect that I stole a colt and and have him stabled
in the bathroom of this two up two down brain. Some days when
I'm lonely he reaches me by neighing and it stays in my eardrums
reverberating so forgive me but at times I can't make out a word
you're saying and every day I get these surges of exhilaration
thinking how this chunky white-legged creature is the perfect
demonstration of how much I think you're worth and I can't stop
myself from visiting him, I creep out quite often now and I'm not
even missing the bits of our shared life I give him.

Horse Latitude

What do you mean when you affix
those phrases to the flare of a nostril
or the grease-warm feel of neck muscles
hidden under a rough knotted mane?

Why spell out this anatomy
not your own? It's there one way
or another and unlike some expectant
lover it doesn't pace and wait
for you to name it.

Tell me what can fetlock signify
when the joint's own leg, own heart
own foot don't know the term?

The sound, low and secret,
a mare makes to her foal holds
no gospel, no prophesy however hard
you try and even as you describe it
resonating in your blood, your bones
your womb; laden though it is
it doesn't speak for you.

You search out the music in hoof on grass,
the scratch of teeth on another's back,
but I say even if that whiskered lip
responds in kind, it's on instinct
not affection
not connection
and that's fine.

And I've been groomed to use this tongue
these fingers and to never second guess it
I don't share your need to hear the music
from a hoof that doesn't know
the tune it's playing.

I grew with them, can catch the wildest,
calm the highest strung
though I no longer have the need to;
I know horses
and they know nothing
or very little of me
and that is as it should be.

In Anger, Hope and Undefeatable Love

For Bety Carino—Murdered 27th April 2010 Oaxaca Mexico.

Cowards, same story
hope defeats you.
Plagiarists stealing
scripts you didn't write
just parrots, but deadly,
see hope? You kill it,
with whatever is to hand
then find what you murdered
was only one strand
of a many headed parade of
laughing dreamers and seekers.
People, who show their faces
disregarding baseless illusions
separating classes and races—
we dream of better and give you night sweats.
Cowards.

With threats of no more
than a good example
bare armed cheap workers
land guardians, peasant farmers
and the very idea of a world
where we are their keepers brothers
or lovers and they ours,
scares you.
Cowards

You'll choke on that fear of songs,
embraces and clearly shown faces.
Kill us? Would that you wouldn't
would that you'd join us instead,
but still we'll bury our dead
then return to face you

with hope and imagination
again
and again
and again...

Shut Up

I'd lay the corpses face down
muted and neat
then lay their ghosts
I wouldn't have their swollen feet
swing from ceilings
where I sleep
I wouldn't get sidetracked
by grief when
it wasn't really me
who lost, if I was no one.

The violated wouldn't ever
speak out loud to me on streets,
in car parks or on
the stacked-up aisles
of supermarkets packed
with things I'd never need
or be entitled to, if I was no one.

I'd never have to listen
to women either dead or walking,
insisting that I spare them
my sympathy, telling me
that I too have traded
in their currency
and bartered flesh for shelter
for protection, if I was no one.

This mercenary marching army
of the dead, the raped, the sold
all chanting; spare us
your sympathy sweetheart
our debts were paid in spades
of heavy earth dead-sounding

on the empty unmarked
graves of who we could have been
or were, they'd never
get away with it, if I was no one.

And this racket
of the never thanked,
the live-but-left, who I've never
countered never challenged
and still won't, they'd get no hearing.
They'd shut up;
if I was no one I'd sleep alone
but these days
there's just no talking to them.

The Centre Never Held Anything Anyway

For Kevin Higgins and WB Yeats

I'm not in the business of accepting accolades for having
a non shrink-wrapped vacuum-packed world view truth is
the centre's never held anything only both contending edges can
so you can burn me with all those other witches if you think
anything we have worth anything was granted on the whims
of jaded marionettes nothing here in middle ground appeared
magic-wanded free of cost demands foretell supply so if you
call me demanding I'll be complimented when these days free choice
means choosing your conditioning to stop you resisting then
there's no convincing me that this system is the best for most
or any: with nearly half of humanity existing toothless I'll gladly
be reactionary and if it's dogmatic to say I don't buy this then
I'll bark it for a lifetime the way town mongrels howl out their existence.

Bleeding Horses

All these bleeding horses,
you can't hear yourself think
with the endless racket of their
whinnying last-gasp I'm here—
I'm here call and answer chants
and Helen pet, sheath those Trojans
in your blouse there are no incognitos
in this herd so unless you're prone
to necrophiliac urges, move along
love there's nothing to see here,
and that coach and four is less than
apocalyptic with its coconut shell
hoof-beats, not spellbound either
these beasts are walking cold.
I think I'll name the deadest Ozymandias
he's no stalking horse this colt
concealing sure death for a snipe or grouse
behind his shoulder, no, there are no birds
and what's more no hands, just a mess
of nerve endings congealing, but still standing
and he's getting ridden good and proper
then put up wet, by a straw man
who hasn't a notion that he's flogging
a pulse deficit, he'll be shocked and awed
to to see haunches buckling, forelegs kneeling
as his mount sprawls sideways
on the turf, what's worse though
is how all these stables' doors are closed,
with the stupid bolted
nags still in them.

She said some days she'd like to live on a long distance night bus

Up three steps no baggage on board
drivers change shifts and in the front seat
the sleepless last stop tourist sits,
faces changing beside her from each
dead night station, she forms an alliance;
shares swear words when other drivers swerve
into the path, then shares driver's elation at escaping.
Oaxaca, lit station, the bus is a moth, roadblock,
immigration don't check the white skinned
just chat, 'Irlanda—muy lejos, qué haces aqui?
Estás solo?' Confusion, masked by politeness
masked by darkness, station.
Tears from girls, outside the glass
hugging a brother going north, blip town,
Arriaga; lights drew them in. Discussing:
the US and why she's not married with a widescreen
TV-carrying border-swimmer returning.
Legs asleep, mind flitting not grasping, dim scenery
passing bodily functions suspended, truck stop.
Smoking outside driver shares Churros
with his one member alliance, makes sure
she goes to the drivers section to eat
asks why she's not married is she travelling alone?
Back in, darkness ahead. Discusses:
road building, night driving, exchange rates,
and why she's not married with soft spoken
hard handed tar macadam ganger, working
two weeks on two weeks off. Tuxtla, he's off.
Replaced. Discusses: meta physics and
why tourists always read with nervy Honduran,
asks why she's not married and 'no le gustan los niños?'
Tourists like reading. This is a fact now.
Rain sparks the windscreen, seat beside's vacant

last three stops driver's gone garrulous
mission nearly complete three towns with no one
Four AM, black sky greying last lights pull them in
and it's baggage back, hand-shakes, real world.

Mid Day on the Camino

For Noeleen and Maria

—Se hace camino al andar

If you want to know something about yourself stay out there
at midday. At noon on the Camino, there's no one, the pilgrims
all scared off the trail by a high shadow-less sun are lurking
in dim churches or restaurants nursing their chaffings and ailments.
Those who walk, the real ones I mean, not day trippers, escape artists
not worshippers or those people with careers to go back to:
I'm talking about the scarce few who came for the walk of it
for the loss of it, for the no going back of it, they know
that at midday even if the the back of your neck and your hairline
get torched, and there's no shade for any living thing they know
that at midday there's air there, and life for your feet you can move
with liquidity, you can walk—unaccompanied.

At midday sun and exposure scare even your own shadow away,
steal off with the pulse from your wrists, your neck, from your brain
they bake your thoughts 'til all you are is the hot air in your lungs
and your step, the life in it. There's only your feet where you place them
and you, and it's a 'you' that gets more indistinct each foot fall but at four
in the evening when the pilgrims return there'll be shadows, whole crowds
of them trail blazing. The pilgrims come here to find themselves but
you should know, there are others who come to get lost.

Melancholic Revolution

(San Cristobal de Las Casas 2009)

If you could sell the last light of evening
from a mountain town this magic-wand shine,
that forces every jaded thing to glitter
would be the most expensive.
The sadness of a fading revolution
against the glare of our too harsh world
has an irresistible poignancy
and we walk the wand lit streets for it.
Melancholic.

In the square a refugee camp
of mountain families displaced by violence
has a fire I can't help wanting to share
and it's washed in strains of music
from the marimba bandstand
but the soldiers eat ice creams
with machine guns shining
and laugh as dozens of tent-city children
spin till they're dizzy and fall on the flagstones
laughing too, with flames of day
on their skin. The mothers, watching
indulgent, won't be made victims in this light
and it's hard not to think all's as it should be
on a day that hurts like this.

False Walls

Snap the padlock of a desultory chain
closed against no one,
watch tail lights receding,
the pick-up lurching away
down the packed earth track,
watch, until it reaches the river bend
under pines blotting out the night sky:
now you're alone.

A lean young dog called Wolf
harebrained and demented chases
his tail in circles up ahead
on the rutted road. At this hour
it's just a dark flatness holding faint
memories in your nostrils of its daytime
earth-red smell.

Walk to the low roofed house,
no refuge though in warm stone
corralled only by expanses
and oppressive presences:
dark hulks of mountains,
nighttime pines and a dry river bed.
For you, the village two hours away
is as incredible as God.

And though you have your beacon of light
in all this thick space, the beam
from the window turns the two hundred year old
worn-smooth shelter to an uneasy prop.
You'll stay outside that night
not sleeping on the still warm path,
your back against the useless wall,
an arm over the dog's matted coat.

Dawn greys, when they come
will be instants, defeated by savage
high blues, burnt earth
and low black-green valleys.
Preferring to face the suffocation of space
and stars and nothing than fool yourself
with meaningless walls
it will be a week or more
before you can sleep inside.

Walking Naked

I met a naked girl walking
and I told her sometimes
I go driving in the afternoon
to nowhere in particular
just roads is all
but she didn't know what drive
or road were.

I told her sometimes that old
rootlessness saw me giving head
to men in raincoats in shop doorways
on deserted rainy streets in cities
I wasn't even from
I thought in her nudity she
wouldn't judge me
and sure enough she asked me
about the raincoat but not
what head was.

I told her about fast food and sloth
about magazines and books
she knew books she said and procured
a missionary's bible
from somewhere below
her pocket-less hide
I wanted to know where she'd
stowed it but, also,
I wanted to be well thought of
so I just said; well sort of–
that sort of is a book.

Then I told her about singing and music
but she knew and said she'd learned some songs
and sang them while I listened

I felt a craving and misplaced it knowing
ice-cream was incongruous
to our situation but faced
with explaining cows
and refrigeration, I gave up.

She said sickness was everywhere
so I told her about medicine
but she took me to be the cure
for waterborne infections
and diseases of the elders
and when I said you overestimate me
she said believe believe
and I said knowing something existed
didn't mean I could orchestrate it
and I tried describing processes
for qualifying and I said
there were such things as education
and examinations and she said
ridiculous and I said believe me I know,
and knew it was me who was overdressed
for the occasion not her
who was stark naked.

Small-time

that fat moon at the window
doesn't spread her white night
fakery for the likes of me,
those tides set their stall to
pull on other amazons while
I wear pairs of trousers with
six or eight inches dragging
at my heels redundant for
lengths I'll never go to,
block-built dictionaries mock
how few of their charges I engage,
while florid fantasies skirt by me
spotting that in the most inner
of my innards I couldn't stretch
their florescent boundaries.
I'm bestowed with a low centre
and no gravity, but I do hold tenure
on this squatting streetscape,
and in this canvas of the near-fetched
I find there's plenty.

Instructions on Evolution for all Apes

After Kafka

Some pointers for your impending personification: quit
your prevarication, cease and desist, we will socialise you
whether you concur or resist, so halt those hesitations,
walk upright, denounce primitive leanings, resist scratching
itchings in public, perform regular ablutions, have recourse
to implements immediately, don't dwell on your lost caves
or kindreds, that's the spirit. Forthwith submit to education
memorise new obligations think in terms of employability,
employ reason, defy logic, render instinct redundant promptly
familiarise yourself with tick and tock and henceforth measure
seasons with them, cover expanses with cloth or tarmac, practice
consumption till its firmly embedded, sleep from now on,
on elevated benches ensure you familiarise yourself with repentance
and guilt, hoard things for use at your leisure, ignore nostalgic tendencies
and should they descend unbidden, historic revisionism will help
to moderate their effects, okay then have you finished? Excellent—
please accept my congratulations on your personification.

My Kind of Men

I grew up with them,
not your office shirted
gelled-hair aftershave type;
fishermen with thick hair full of salt
dealing men, 'living on their wits
and getting pretty thin,' men
with codes no bank has ever
heard of for behaviour
and weird ethics no judge
could hope to understand.
They had phrases,
'humpy cow, humpy calf',
'bright girl wanted' or
'a minute's thinking is worth
an hour of running'.
They had ropes, jump leads
and old long-used wrenches,
dockets and empty cigarette
packets on dashboards.
They made sounds
of fraternity; 'a shout
is a great man when you're lifting'
shared wordless noises to unite them.
These guys could spot each
other at the counter
in the takeaway, or on
the ferry to 'Le Harve'
in butchered accents,
they had driven loads of oranges
from Spain to the communist bloc,
and applied a dealer's logic
to everything they saw there.
They pulled drowning
people out of caves,
shot dogs that wanted it,
tolerated nothing in others
and made sounds,
approaching conversation.

Aquí Estamos en la Amistad

('here we are in friendship' for Ana)

For bringing Gramsci and hope
to private school students
those products of all you oppose,
for not once pointing out
that my cynicism is cheap
and a cop-out from someone
who still has a choice
or that the questions here
can be die or resist not
which brand of dogma to preach.

For knowing without asking
that my abstracted reactions
to this mounting list of slain
are refusals to daytrip through
someone else's heartbreak
but not holding it against me,
for never seeming to resent
my one foot on dry land
when no one here has standing room
for realising that I see
a harsh beauty here, because
I found hope amongst all this violence
and gentleness in someone
who still dares to believe
and that despite all this;
aquí estamos en la Amistad.

Didn't Get It

Education, they asked me, what had I studied and where?
So I told them; once my job was to sell as many
pigs in pokes as I was able and try to buy none
I was schooled to know the day you couldn't sell something
is the day you should head on out and buy some.
People I knew, picked reeds on river banks to sell
for thatching or gathered winkles at low tide
on Grattan beach and Bearna for Frenchmen
they'd never seen to eat, they knew where holly
with berries, could be had in December but only
passed that knowledge on to family members and me.
They bought wrought iron gates from old estates
called other junk 'antique' then found customers for it
as sometimes I did, and what we couldn't sell we'd swap;
anything to be dealing, we knew exchange rates to the decimal
so we could trade across borders we'd never crossed and
when they spoke in generalisations about whole nations
saying; Englishman's honest but you've to watch the cash
with Spaniard – I learned.

They bought knacker-horses and old worn-out cattle,
or show ponies and pedigree livestock. It didn't matter,
as they said, it's the same pound you get whether
it's high class or lower and I found that true myself,
any time I went to spend some. We bought, sold or swapped
trailers, lorries and old tractors anything at all so long as
there was a chance of a punter after, and I knew, as they did,
that you must never spoil a sale for a dealer, there isn't any luck
from that sort of trade, but if you help a sale being made
you're due some commission and when you see someone
buying something you've been chasing, the right thing to do
is leave them to it then offer a quick profit straight after
on dealer's honour they'll have to take it, or pay you
the same jingle to not ask them. So I answered: here and there,
around about, that's where I got my education and they said
thanks very much for your time Ms Clancy.
Next Please.

Full of Useless Words

Here I'm not so full
of useless words
I can't take refuge
in spectaculars of
verbosity
I have to black
or white it,
say it as I mean it,
but I have enough
to say give me
your hand and I'll hold it
and like a light
left on for a sleeping child
at night it leaves all
the pitch black space
outside irrelevant
and I can dance like
dust within
the beam of it.

Llena De Palabras Inútiles

Aquí no estoy tan llena
de palabras inútiles
no puedo refugiarme
en espectáculos de verbosidad
tengo que blanquear o oscurecer
decirlo sin rodeos
pero tengo suficiente
para decir dame
la mano y me la agarro
y como una luz que se deja prendida
para un niño dormido
de noche deja irrelevante
al espacio profundo negro
y puedo bailar como
polvo dentro
de su rayo.

Walking Fear Dubh (The Devil)

She said it results from seeking approval
whilst simultaneously refusing to be
judged by the standards of others and
really the only answer to that is
what the fuck would she know about it?
I got better advice from a man who once
kicked his pregnant wife in the stomach
he told me: it's like this, there's a road and
you walk it, if you don't like the bed then
think, before you turn down the covers.
Of the easy way out he said he'd never
give anyone to say that he'd done it and
once you know that there's no other solution:
you're stuck bringing every bastard you've been
along with you, so before you create one it's better
he reckoned to think of how you'll listen to Fear Dubh
when he's walking that long road beside you.

Tomcatting and You

For my two favourite misogynists

How you love these confessionals where you get to twist knives in your
own wounds and I supply fresh blades whenever they're needed, drama
being the opposite of surrender, those ones where I walk tightropes
of I do 'cause I can, shifting between five portions a day, 2.2 children
not dropping litter and careful economising on my production of CO_2,
by using your body for warmth, or tomcatting; selling snake oil I don't
even have for three times its value somewhere wedged between night
and the day somewhere light on an iris forces tear ducts into excess
production, where consequences are odysseys with lives of their own
dominos clicking down, one down, one down and you ask if I love you?
That's hardly original there, it's no more than a misnomer, a brown
spreading melanoma on the skin of extinction except when for contrast
I'm craving the melancholia of frost on a hardworking morning, craving
from a distance, from out here in the warp of my gambler's bazaar,
where prices are haggled but never paid where the good-ly are us who
succeed in weaving webs of attraction around us and specialise in
seducing then walking away even if it's only ourselves we have our way
with and you ask if this is home for me then retreat and regroup, fearing
you've gone that one step too far when I could be prowling all night
selling some decrepit rescue option on a hedonism so tainted it makes
itself art out where the artless are poison and no contracts have weight,
these rivulets, these streams, between the bought and the sold, are
so easy to step over, and then there's you in a kitchen or at the premier
of the film of your life and it's got me in it and mine likewise has you as
the built in risk factor without whom this drama would shed its compulsion.
It's not pretty this tomcatting: would it not be best if we left some
of these questions unanswered?

Plea from a no longer existing nation

This poor house is all forlorn looking, I swear it's shrunk
it's full of scraped pot-bottoms dolefully reminiscing about
me washing off the shrapnel from your various burnt offerings,
the chipped mugs and half a dozen odd socks you couldn't
bring yourself to part with don't seem to fit in without you
and the shoes all three sizes bigger than I could ever wear
keep bickering at me from beneath the bed, they say it's
my fault and won't hear different and in the front room
the magazines are devastated on the sofa, especially Vanity Fair;
I tried a flick through to reassure it and it just said, yea baby
like you even care and the books well we won't talk about
the books or how that postcard from Trotsky's house now
seems permanently off kilter and those plastic joined up
Frida eyebrows you got me for my birthday have adopted
a scowl even though they don't have a mouth to hang it on,
and I know you'll find this disturbing but I thought I'd better
tell you your Tito fridge magnet has succumbed to a persistent
depression not fitting for the father of a no longer existing nation
and we're all stuck here together not sure how exactly we're related
and I'm trying to placate them, you know treat them gently
see I understand they're suffering but it seems they're all full of
a justified resentment and maybe you could settle it, would there be
any chance you'd drop by to see them, if you happen to be passing?
It's for them I'm asking...

Riot Act

You turned the last drip of evening sinister, unattractive
you turned it quicksilver and left it pulsing like a blister
on a mercurial city of murdered graffiti-boy's scrawls
and wealth deflected, like the light you refracted
ten minutes before when you matter of fact-ed, all bets off
promises retracted, took our history, ransacked it,
took the future and attacked it over margaritas neither
could pay for or swallow, you left me space cadetted
lump in the throated as I walked it out past the town park
with dogs on the street barking it, past shops night break
had gap toothed, censored redacted, you left me with
my fucking heart looted and then said I over reacted.

Don't Think I Won't

This time when I leave it will be final
your closed skies and sullen weather
won't drag me back, we've so little
scope here for imagination
our wet cardboard self regard
can't make amends for days spent
drinking—in trees, stones, turloughs
and empty winter beaches
as if they stood for something
finding that they in fact
are nothing more or less than nature
and no one here stands for anything,
we are too busy self deprecating

and what ties I have here
consist of shared commiserations
about our inability to make a change
not from music on the streets
or attempts and failures
nothing heartfelt gets expressed
in our suffocating culture and
at least if I don't find wild inspiration
somewhere, I'll have walked away
from my arranged marriage
with this unforgiving country.

She Takes Me Back

for this Atlantic Rock we live on

for the thirteenth time,
not with meekness or resignation
she just takes possession
there's no way she'll get aggrieved
at my fleeting passions
for some other's cheap displays
or how their scent lingers on my skin,
no, she'll never even ask about
my attempts to shake her off
she knows they won't hold a candle
to the grip she has on me, she's sure
she's in each and every thought I have
she's the watch tower I'm looking out from
but she has no need of me for anything.

If she thinks I'm a fool for suffocating
then I'm her fool on this clear day
when my frosted breath can travel
across endless sea she's streaked out
in brassy lines of sun stretching further
than my eyes can see, at night
she puts on a high crisp display of stars
that shrink me to minuteness
and spell out; fool,
if you think you'd leave.

For the Living and the Dead

The **Truth** is every ending pre-determined **Truth** is washing never ending lines of dishes, working **Truth** is every lie you told each intricate fiction and it's your blurtings **Truth** is all those spectres that exist only in your wildest drunken ravings **Truth** is every act you've ever made on instinct every figment **Truth** is every one you ever loved and those you fucked but didn't **Truth** is Terrence Wheelock getting his young life beaten in Store street station **Truth** is every reluctant surrender and it's resistance **Truth** is Omagh and saying it and there's **Truth** in every unjust occupation **Truth** is in the bureaucrats, the grafters, **Truth** is Rachel Corrie, all those dreamers **Truth** is every deportee each exile who sings a cloying lament for passing **Truth** is finished in the spectacle and there's **Truth** in every single new beginning **Truth** is in your here and now your socks your window cleaning **Truth** is in the rules and structures in weeds obsessed with sprouting **Truth** is in the pot you burned as much as every gourmet dinner served **Truth** is in the poems you kept and those in your waste basket **Truth** is in the glib and mellow oldies station and the things your intellect can't fathom **Truth** is in the market for buyers, sellers, unrequited it's the hustle **Truth** is in the slipstream and it lurks in every trite denial **Truth** is in the cast offs, in your hoarding **Truth** is in the secrets and it's flamboyant on the billboards **Truth** is on the busy streets there walking **Truth** lives on deserted lanes and dies in sheltered corners **Truth** is in the fibres where your DNA's deciphered **Truth** is in the learning more even the forgetting **Truth** is **Truth** and there's no true thing that doesn't end nor even any lie that lasts **Truth** is bloated with its own importance when the **Truth** is it doesn't matter because every single thing is **TRUE**.

A relative newcomer to the poetry world, SARAH CLANCY has been writing poetry for just over two years. During this time she has had the good fortune to be shortlisted for several poetry prizes including the Listowel Collection of Poetry Competition and the Patrick Kavanagh Award. Her first themed collection, *Stacey and the Mechanical Bull*, was published by Lapwing Press Belfast in December 2010 and a further selection of her work was published in June 2011 by Doire Press. Her poems have been published in *Revival Poetry Journal, The Stony Thursday Book, The Poetry Bus, Irish Left Review* and in translation in *Cuadrivio Magazine* (Mexico). She was the runner up in the North Beach Nights Grand Slam Series 2010 and was the winner of the Cúirt International Festival of Literature Grand Slam 2011. She has read her work widely at events such as Cúirt and as a featured reader at the Over the Edge reading series in Galway, the Temple House Festival, Testify, Electric Picnic, O Bheal and at the Irish Writers' Centre, she was an invited guest at the 2011 Vilenica Festival of Literature in Slovenia and in Spring 2012 a poem of hers received second prize in the Ballymaloe International Poetry Competition. Email: clancy_sarah@hotmail.com